DORA / LORA

LARISSA SHMAILO

Unlikely Books
www.UnlikelyStories.org
New Orleans, Louisiana

Dora / Lora

Eighteen Dollars US

ISBN: 978-1-959377-01-6

Library of Congress Control Number: 2022948279

Unlikely Books
www.UnlikelyStories.org
New Orleans, Louisiana

DORA / LORA

Хай живе Україна!
Long live Ukraine!

THE ORDER IN WHICH THEY APPEAR

LORA

Preface:
Spectacle is the Fundamental Principle of Fascist Art

Come, hide with me from
their violence in the vi-
olets. They're soon gone.

AMOR FATI

As a girl, I dreamt of riding my bicycle until I was lost and could find my way home only with difficulty – the challenges of space were denied me. I consoled myself with the old ponies who dragged the carts for children's rides at the quarter-mile boundary of things I knew.

In my backyard, a 12-x-12-foot square of green with a magical garage, I focused on the bees, the yellow-black and working brown. Stung much, I took it as the price of friendship. My grandmother's roses, six rich bushes, hid in a pink one an iridescent Japanese beetle, shimmering phosphorescent green.

I didn't know the metamorphic dandelions I loved were weeds; I never will believe it, nor of vetch. These are the prejudices of stupid people who need to be told what to love, because I always knew; even my mano a mano *mama knew. Because she told me about death ("Everything can be fixed except . . . ") and showed me the flowers on my Babushka's, her mother's grave, I forgive her everything. I do not forget how they yelled at one another, only knew that that was unimportant, that the flowers, brought or grown there on the grave, were.*

My rooster walked proudly on the grass, living his short life with me from an Easter chick to death on Long Island. He died defending chickens from dogs, my mother said, but really was sold for Sunday dinner; the point being, it could not be fixed.

Why did I say my rooster died? That was, I believe, before I knew death and its fixity. I learned the lesson of the dead bees on my backyard lawn, my yellow and black brethren, vital, alarming one moment, little appendages curled upward, inert and stiff, the next.

With Chef Boyardee and lunch, with breakfast and Babushka's apple cake came the Holocaust and bees and Stalin and Happy the Cock: Death, inevitable, never escaped, only postponed, heroic and tragic, always to be honored.

Worms, so plentiful, wriggling after a rain: my amor fati *known to me even then, to be the little cornflowers and earth-munching worms, and a part of a tree, and an element, carbon for photosynthesis, an atom for someone to breathe in, this my assured eternity.*

ASYLUM

Psychiatry is the monologue of reason to madness – Michel Foucault

We walk
naked down the street and
upon water.

A false light, that of images you
project, sees
agitation, melancholia, passion,
spasm.

Separation,
confinement is needed
(fear of what we will bear).

Board, then,
my *stultifera navis*,
but mind the gap.

Come where there is
no foothold, where
things sway.

We who have drunk
the salt
our heads touched
by Jesus

will show you the
rue true meaning
of asylum.

&

My love, I see myself in a fur coat lying face down, drunk,
on the floor of the subway train, one heel lost, & I feel a
hardened man raping me, my virgin soul frost, & awards
are easy, mama says, & they may elect and choose you, but,
they don't know you, Ms. Boss, & my father says that I am
sexy & the time after that is lost & I know I am fat,
that I cost, & before she dies, mama says she wishes
I was never born, my death in my mother's eyes, crossed,

but my love, see this chasm & wall here & be brave for me,
come swim the swamp around me & trust it is not within me,
or if it is, come love this swamp creature until it is drained,
and look at the dead in the moat, for here they will remain,
& sit here, still, with me & I will haltingly explain
I still love, beyond barbs, beyond wounds, beyond pain.

ABORTION HALLUCINATION

In the corner of the basement where my father used to lie I
watch, interested, as the snake
grows larger and more menacing I am
taken slightly aback but remember him remember that I like
handling snakes and smile
and as always he softens grows smaller
becomes a hippopotamus I have won again I have stared him down
made him warm
and the Nile gives up its life to me
animals carnivorous and calm come home to me
two by two

I watch for the longest time
until the largest fills the window with his face
black as light
Agnus Dei

for this man's baby for this man's baby for this man's baby
came the flood.

Anna Karenina

Oh, Merezhkovsky, she was a mare
too good for her rider; a man bare
of fine temperament, riding her hard,
playing her roughly, like a cheat's card,
leaving her broken.

Vronsky, sad: beauty was given you, cad.
And you lived like a man only because of her,
you, a creature dead in soul, and she, you cur,
destroyed, no longer fit to ride:
You might have loved her still, your bridle bride.

Anna Karenina: #MeToo

Ah, Merezhkovsky: to you I was a mare
ridden badly by a man; and because of him,
his error, I had to be destroyed. And Lev, my dear:
You never gave me my own voice, you didn't dare.
What did I talk about when I did talk, after all:
Abortion with Dolly? Every damn thing
Vronsky did, that I did better? The problem
was not that I was sexual: (Men, you
count on that.) The problem was that
I was smart. But sexual women must be killed;
All the books attest to that.

Merezhkovsky permeates the consciousness
of Slavic scholars, is the Anna story, still,
but I fault you most, Lev. You knew, soon
into the novel, that the problem was not one woman
and one man; it was all women, all men. You had
Vronsky climb in society, while I—damn, I even
knew more about horses than him! I was
the scarlet woman, though our offence was the same.

Did I abandon my child? Or did a martinet
bar me from him? *Ah, she holds Vronsky back!*
Ah, the guilt!

Oh, there is no talking to you.
You sent me the dream
that haunted your ruling-class sleep,
a peasant with an iron,
the proletariat that said, fuck you
and your landlord's way of life.
You killed me with the railroad built for you,
by them. Because you "had to."
Where was your *Resurrection* then?
You repudiated *Karenina*, it's true,
but you abandoned me to my fate.
And so, Lev, I still struggle,
a century and a half later,
to have my story told.

CIS BOOM TRANS

Cis boom trans, yes, I'm a man
within a girl, the neurons whirl
that way. You secretly want me
in your toilet, badly; I can be your
mom *and* dad. What kind of nurture
will my nature bring? Call me a
curio for you, my inflections an
enticement, my infections to be
damned. Transman, what I have
to do to be myself, what I posit
out of the closet, the closed can't
know, no, understand.

THIS IS THE RUPTURE OF HEART

This is the rupture of heart; love's sharp scalpel will cut mine apart.
Only a surgeon could see how to operate so well on me.
This is the intricate pain, come dissecting my frog hurt again.
Eros is clinically bold, and a professional, totally cold.

Catrain

Vagina, labial diner!
Penis, vaginal miner!
Your wife with my husband:
Ptosic shiner!

FALL OF ICARUS

If they were my white legs
Entering the foam unseen;

If I plunged headfirst as around me
Commerce, sex, the great ocean and

The fruits of the field
Proceeded and saw me not;

If I never completed my father's maze;
If the minotaur flayed my flesh;

If lovers wooed and never gazed at me;
If historians never uttered my name;

If I had to live in poverty, in debt, in prison;
If the whole world damned my soul:

Still I would, still I would, still I would
Fly as close as I could to the sun
And with my last breath mock the sheep.

PERSONAL THEOLOGY

There are no angels,
there are these angles.

Your nonexistence—
it exists?—far or near?

You have no control,
only your next breath.

(Will you have the last
one next?) Crestfallen,

now is the nadir, now
is your peak (or pique).

Uncomfortable everywhere in life, like a stray cur, homeless in your soul, you wait like a dog to be walked.

And yet, you are a sunflower, open, spiral, connected by mysterious mathematics to the stars, as far as Andromeda.

So, there is no Big Daddy in the sky, not here or on Andromeda. Is it so terrible to be mortal, finite? Would you read an endless book, watch a droning movie with no end?

Yes, but . . . no, the universe is magical as is, more magical than a theographical library of Absolutes.

It lies on its side, an infinite lemniscate, receptive to all, even unbelievers, is infinite without an Infinite.

Your atoms will continue (you will not), but they will be part of trees and rabbits and soil and stars, as far as, perhaps, Andromeda.

You dance like wheat, like the aurora borealis, like a radio signal from Andromeda, like a magnetic dynamo moving mountains.

You and yours are the atomic bond, your stars fuse hydrogen to make helium, all the elements, all, are within you and about you and are yours, an infinite chemistry. Why do you need a God for this?

RULES OF REFLECTION 2

for John Ashbery

The right hand **bigger than the head *thrust*** at the viewer and *swerving easily away,* as though to protect what it ADVERTISES. *Fur,* muslin, coral ring run together in a movement (*filling pregnant concavity with a convex **shove***).

Chiefly his reflection, of which the portrait   Chiefly his reflection, of which the portrait
Is the reflection, of which the portrait   Is the reflection, of which the portrait
Is the reflection once removed.   Is the reflection once removed

THE MIRROR

O

in which I **see *Parmigianino***
HEAR Vasari and they are the reflections which alone
HEAR and **see** the poet and his unequal hybrid *READ.*
(NB: What is accessibility - why have it when there are mirrors looking upon mirrors looking mirthfully at looking glasses instead?)

**ART IS REFLECTION ART IS INFECTION ART IS INSURRECTION
ART IS DIRECTION ART IS ERECTION**

The glass chose to reflect only what he saw a recurring wave of arrival.

ART IS ARRIVAL:

The swimming soul seeks the shore of eyes that see it, that safety, happily captive there.

THE MIRROR: The words are only speculation (from the Latin *speculum,* "mirror"): **a monocular spectacle with double vision, this love.**

When light is reflected by convex mirrors, a virtual image is formed

& the image of an object can be found from a single point

>< . >< . >< . >< . >< FIN >< . >< . >< . >< . >< .

SIBYL

With frenzied mouth uttering things not to be laughed at, unadorned and unperfumed, yet reaches to a thousand years with her voice by aid of the god.
—Heraclitus

The reader is dismayed: the novel is replete
with a plot in disarray and a hero quite effete.
The theme is death and chaos and the sum of man's defeat;
But the *Times* proclaims that it sells well and claims that it's a treat.

The movie is quite long, a *chagrin et pitié;*
the acting isn't strong and the editing a *melée* . . .

STOP.
THESE WORDS ARE NOT MY WORDS
MY WORDS WILL NOT AMUSE YOU
MAKE YOU SMIRK.

MY WORDS
WILL NOT TELL YOU
WHAT ART IS
OR IS NOT (IT IS ALL).

MY WORDS
ARE GIVEN TO YOU
WHETHER YOU ARE READY TO RECEIVE THEM
OR NOT.

MY WORDS
MAKE YOURS THE ASH
FROM WHICH PHOENIXES ARISE.

I AM YOUR LOGOS, THE WORD MADE FLESH.

I AM WHAT YOU LONG FOR AND FEAR.

I AM WHAT I AM.

HEAR ME: I AM HERE TO TELL YOU
THAT I AM YOU.

New Life 7 - Mistranslation of Joseph Brodsky with Addenda

Clearer, clearer

now: the alphabet sings,

calling "Betsy," "Abrahim,"

and I, grayer, saner now,

ring a voice without tears.

I wait for a train that

will never come, wait for

that degree of beauty,

iron-cast, ironclad, sure.

Does my sail judge

the horizon, or does

the horizon judge my sail?

Older, I leave aspiration

to the sea, keeping only

my breath, this one here.

Perhaps six, nine breaths

from now I will be dead,

or ten. Respire, aspire.

expire. Tired.

What meaning does

legacy have for the

un-resurrected dead?

What few readers are left?

Betsy, Abrahim, the rest

less. The alphabet sings only

to me. War's cast iron

grates surround me,

the vulgar scions, b-b-b-b

k-k-k-k.

DORA

A Preface Assumes

A view from above, a collection of language surfaces;
membrane: scattering, oblivion, waste,
the extinction of the voice, an obscene scream.
Vvedensky, Blanchot, Bataille, the deceased Kondratiev,
memory and some kind of incomprehensible responsibility,
delineation and erasure, the pornography of disappearances:
Orpheus, a cloud of crumbling powder. A reading that can only be imagined.
A mask of winking irony, or, say, tolerant correctness,
someone who silently whispers into the strands of someone's hair.

SCHOOLING

The motions of children
of courts

Carlight
industrial prolegomena

Eradicated Ovids
fast loose change

Rivers of tar, of cars, of tattered water
leave the driving to us

"I love you."
"Don't talk to me that way."

Resistance is futile

Under the spreading chestnut tree
God's joke

Come to me
my mitochondrial baby

I sing a song of mouse elf

Heidegger, Heidegger everywhere
and not a stop to think

Resistance is utile

In the conifer stands, Artemis's breath
she doesn't work here any more

Fuck utopia
More burnings

Resistance is a drink
for those who think,
a meal for those who feel

Jumping off premises
the white cliffs are over

Tolstoy: "Turgenev;
can-can; boring."

Dig a whole
for decapitated Anna

The peasant become
proletarian, iron clad
then fat.

Did I arouse you, America?
Good. Coke is life.

Your jeans become genes
the eugenics

Not to interrupt the show, but
do you still know
how to pleasure yourself?

Kompromat

Kremlin lawyer, come close,
especially in summer;
I want a secret channel to you,
ambassador to my heart.

Collude with me nearly, dear,
for, *liubov moi,* what is dirt?
One op's oppo is another's
conspiracy of the heart.

Tovarishch, dossier me close,
most in summer. Come and
we'll leak when we want,
be hotel tarts of the heart.

Comrade, you can't stop my heart's
treason if its reason is you.

AMERICAN LIFE

mama

soma

chemo

coma

mama . . . ?

Tetragrammaton

FUCK

Exegesis: The source of all life,
hence, these four characters
of the unnameable divine.

Cloud in Stained Panties

America, cloud in stained panties,
I have walked your streets waiting
for you, wailing for you. Porn star
of my dreams, beneath your g-string
something's not right, not tight.

Yet, yes, I love your long-lost lap,
your creases deeper than innocence.
I am still asleep, but embrace me,
inadequate, schizophrenic maw:
Your values and valves are mine.

Give me your teat of token trust,
broken rust. Immaternal, never eternal,
you push me, rush me to your cold
sold breast, which crushes me again,
banishes me and vanishes as of old.

CLAD, CLAWED, CLANDESTINE EAGLY PIG

$$f(n) = \begin{cases} 0 & if \quad n = 0 \\ 1 & if \quad n = 1 \\ F(n-1) + F(n-2) & if \quad n > 1 \end{cases}$$

E

I
I
id
eye:
Lie as
eyes lie, I.
Delineating it,
disentangling inclines
in lies; incidentals cast a delicate sign.
Cling in line, eyeing diligent penalties, laws, claws: it's eyes in lies.
Anteceding id, laws distancing 1, clasping ties, inspecting id, an eye, a lie; all ID, and stenciled, penciled eyes.

PLATE HISTRIONICS

He throws a gold-lamé wedding-set saucer
      at me, and spits, "There is no
            global warm-ing."

      Today, Irma evacuates Sarasota as b-
     rother Harvey peers and jeers, Ozymandiu-
s-like, Houston and Florida, look upon me.

A-s th-ese li-nes are bro-ken, so the dream-
      s of cities, and those hamlets and towns a-
         way where we settled to breathe, hear our-
            selves think.

      Cat 5, there is no stronger. An
evil fidget spinner, Irma swirls out of a wet
hell, and I holler CLIMATE CHANGE.

It is the
      imitation
            Wedgewood gravy boat, h-
                e throws that next, jjjjjjjust before she

degree

Look up, the water is rising again; the ocher ocean is

warmer today. The sea mists rise, form grey clouds

named Harvey and Irma and Jose and they reign,

mad royalty, over earth. Hush: The brown waters

rush into tributaries, to rivers, to the troubled chopped

sea, where carbons heat the surface of salt; one degree

1

and it rises hotter, wetter, wilder
whipping waves of wind
winding toward us
a Kitty, Leo, Marie;
a child, looking at the sea
will die today
Noah, alee.

Spectrum Sells Out

Pay for yourself, I said; or you will be full of violet bullet holes.

Ah, *schweinherz*, remember when we used to make love beneath skies of angled light, brighter than sandpaper? The grass, dripping emeralds, did not crumble; even the pissant leaves, stretched like the refracted rubber of your brightly piqued (inaudible)

(I never said you completed any Kantian imperative. I don't bow to the rain. I am not talking about grass because of Neruda or Lorca, viny fellows dripping with tears. I just would like to dialectic with you.)

(inaudible) vermillion kitties with rheumy eyes, roomier than your heart, make me dream of clean and ripened razors.

Orange you glad I didn't say yellow, belly? The spectrum scopes, sells out. Here is my indignant indigo diegesis: Diogenes it.

ADOPTION

I was not a mother until today.
The brand Trump is emblazoned on tents
and abandoned Walmarts.
Nannies wear jackboots, joke as
children cry.
Secretly, at night, children are taken
to undisclosed locations across the nation.
Where are the girls? With
the Roy Moores of the world?
Hear my NO.
Listen, Space Force:
I am the Horta, fighting for my children;
I will drive you from the planet.
Attention, big game hunters:
I am a tigress, risen from extinction,
to protest, protect the little cubs.
I, ordinary woman, with my instincts intact,
the maternal rising in me like a huge blue tide:
watch me topple the Orange Ozymandius.

What you have unleashed can't be
lied to or stopped.
I am more than #me, too;
I am the children, too.

"An old red tree . . ."

An old red tree, dry,
who lusts for wide wet summer
tries to plant a seed.

Frog Prayer

Dark Light, stark Light, take me from the public bog

where I, frog, lurk, waiting for a divine arch

to spark the dog in me.

                In me fight tedium, odium,

banal canals of waste; light, I squat and

slight, rape.

        Slight rape forgiven? Dear God of Frogs:

        Please goad, load me,

take my slippery smoothness, flippery foolishness

away.

A way must be sound: I am wrapped in myself,

trapped in myself. My froggy self longs to produce, create;

but no, I seduce, berate.

Berate me, Tricolored Frog:

Light whose waste product is air, help me,

for as I sit and soak, I croak, I croak.

A Sonnet Affected by Climate Change

The Earth is mud and shale gas, molten magma, metamorphic—
Oh Sis, Oh Bro—and igneous, blast changing in its last tic,
with a heady burst of ozone, all zones, a corpse that ends in water.
Without us, climate will survive, change fast, outlast—Oh Daughter:
The equatorial world endures, we fall, all bone, all copses sick.

Paleoclimatology predicts our fate.
Put the conundrum on another generation's plate?
No, it's now: in Africa, desertification scorches,
torches farmland. (HUNGER!!!!)
And the people learn of a Great Satan, a nation
that throws away food. Do you see
that they will fight because they must?
Whom will they trust? What is terror after
you've watched your child die in the land's rust?

WHEN POETS GET SHOT

Orange: the color of emergency: Trump's *Mein Kampf* has successfully launched. Here come the Nazis, the pedophiles, the "benevolent white supremacists," the wife rapists, men who like their women bruised, the gay bashers who are secret homosexuals. Yes, Nazism has always had to do with violent and non-consensual sex.

Orange prison uniforms for asylum seekers kept hungry and in cramped dirty quarters. Little babies ripped from their mothers (Reference: see *Sophie's Choice*). One thousand five hundred border babies lost, no one knows where they are, probably in sex trafficking (see paragraph 1).

For you and me, orange uniforms? There is no surety that says no, even if you support the Nazis. One day, a Nazi pal will turn you in as gay or part black or disloyal, and there you go to the camps, to the beautiful BASF or DOW or Monsanto chemical gas (Reference: see *This Way to the Gas, Ladies and Gentlemen* by Tadeusz Borowski).

Here will be the reliable cadres of orange prisoners: mentally ill people, all disabled people for that matter, gays and trans, commies (and who's to say that you are not), latinxs, blacks, and uppity women (whom we will keep in the Frauenblock for fun). And you, if you slip up. Or if somebody wants your job. Or just for fun. Oh, and Jews, perhaps after a reprieve, but always, ultimately Jews. (Reference: See Primo Levi, *Survival in Auschwitz*).

Examples:

In 1921, a poet dreaming of his wife and Addis Ababa
is brought before the firing squad and shot.

During World War II in Stalingrad, a clownish writer accused of espionage dies of starvation
trying to eat his prison mattress.

Poets who died in the camps:
Anica Černej
Grażyna Chrostowska
Robert Desnos
Benjamin Fondane
Pavel Friedmann
Peter Hammerschlag
Jakob van Hoddis
Noor Inayat Khan
Max Jacob
Itzhak Katzenelson
Peter Kien
Gertrud Kolmar
Igor S. Korntayer
Henryka Łazowertówna
Yechiel Lerer

Selma Meerbaum-Eisinger

Erich Mühsam

Arno Nadel

Sarah Powell

Moriz Seeler

Augustyn Suski

David Vogel

Ilse Weber

Here in the U.S., it will be me – I will be called a Democrat and hauled to a dark site to be waterboarded, not because I have any information (I don't), just for stupid sadistic fun. There will be a picture of Ivanka Trump on the wall and my torturers will force me to genuflect and pray to her. I mumble lines from my poetry, proud that they have burned me, proud that I have told the truth. Then come the rats . . . .

DORA / LORA

Preface: Crematorium Limerick

My mother said (dear, dearest Mum)
Camp Dora had no crematorium.
Then she said there was, so;
As a guard there she'd know,
But truth-telling just hurt her poor tum.

Dora/Lora

Sing, bride of Ares, of crimes once committed by banal, plain people,
like gangsters who torture and maim, and then tuck their small children in
without qualm: Eichmann, so typical, could not, even at trial, understand
what he did wrong.

And Mama and Papa, survivors of four camps: no traumatic stress; they
just spoke of places where they were young: Kalinivka, and how they first
met (but not the flowering graves there of Jews, those mass graves);
Prymysl, where there was still food (but not the crammed boxcars, bound
for far ghettos); Erfurt—yes, they spoke of Erfurt, where the selections
took place, and where the finest brick crematoria, sturdy, were built. And then
finally, how they came to the Harz mountains, to Nordhausen, where V2 rockets
were built; in the center, camp Dora, where Jews and exhausted prisoners
died in the crematorium, neither bullet nor rope to spare.

Back, look back, Muse: Who was Father, né Nikolai, Papa, then? A felon or a boy?
Who was my Mother, young Zinaida, his wife? A kapo or child? Sing now,
Calliope, sing and bring me to my forbears, and through them, myself.

Outside of Kharkiv, 1933–1942

Father's tough father was *kulak*, had risen in power, was to Stalin
a threat, and was purged, called an enemy, taken one night and shot: *Enemy*.
And my own father became the damned son of an enemy, denied a Red
Army rank and a commission and gun. Before, handsome, carousing with girls,
an important man's son, he drank nights away. Now at the front, Kolya shot!
A spoiled young man till then, spoiled, and now shot! And next, captured
by German troops; starved and war-weary; they closed their eyes, let the boy go.

To where? To a high cornfield, where, hiding, he looked at his wounded left leg and thought.
"*I* am to die here, ay, *I*!" But he made it to Russian terrain, to the Russian front.
Home! And there, new problems waited, a mother, two siblings to feed. And his
father? His mother told how, daily, she stood on the prison lines, waiting for news:
Husband, alive? And then suddenly through a rough window
a subwarden thrust a white, bloody man's shirt with two bullet holes at her, telling her, "Ah,
ah, you are still young, go away, and remarry, forget." Which to Kolya's great relief, she had.

Still, the young man had more troubles: to fight for the Russians? For Stalin who killed
his own father? He thought of the German he had shot, how he looked at his face, very young,
and the worn picture of his girl at his heart. Then, why kill them, why?

Russia's long exploitation, cruel collectivization, Ukraine's many millions dead.
Europe's rich breadbasket, black-loamed Ukraine, now reduced to a starving mass:
How in the 'thirties, small farms were all seized and grain stolen brutally,
stolen by Stalin and Soviet goons. Now a second serfdom, of peasants
who worked their own land as hired hands, or were exiled or shot down;
villages now soulless *kolkhoz*, collective farms. Bad harvests came and there was no grain;
mass death by starvation, bodies in the streets: the *holodomor*, mass death.

Now the damned Russian war; Stalin now called Ukrainians brothers, called them now to
fight the invaders, the Germans troops. Nikolai grimaced, remembered the corpse
of the German; a soldier; how young the man seemed; in his wallet, that
picture of a woman, who would likely be his wife. Why am I fighting him?
Nikolai asked himself. It is the Russians who harmed me. Ukraine should be free, not
a Soviet slave. Nikolai thought of his father, shot in the night, and of Zina, the girl
he'd just met, thin but so pretty, and smart, an *otlichnitsa*, 5-student; Nikolai
never got a 5 in his life. And her father was a scholar, a professor, unjustly imprisoned
and sent to Siberia, exiled there, sentenced to five year's hard labor; why? for wearing
a Ukrainian shirt. And his crime? It was nationalism, the damned Soviets said.
To serve Stalin, that was all now allowed. Love of country, the Ukraine, a crime.
Proudly, the little professor, his lip and short mustache quivering
welcomed the Germans, and argued (and loudly, for all to hear; Zina cried,
Whisper!) that only the German ambassador protested the famine, the theft
of grain, Ukraine's years-long rape by the Soviets. The horrors that the Soviets,

always reported, the murder of Jews, camps in Germany and Poland—this was
Stalin's propaganda, pure lies. Weren't the Soviets Ukraine's true enemies?

Armies swept back, and again, hard across the Ukraine: first the Soviets,
and then the Germans, then Soviets again. Daily, Zina and her father
watched, and, too, were watched. The Soviet spymasters came around,
checking up on their Ukrainian loyalty. Zina suppressed a sad smile.
Boldly, Professor Nikolai Alekseevich spoke. "Go ahead," he said.
"Check away. There is nothing here; you have taken it all. Go on."
After the state – read Russian – policemen had left, a wan Zina spoke.
Father, I have met a boy, a Nikolai like you, his father was
 purged. And his family suffers from Stalin like us; can he come to call?"

"Ach, my dear daughter, be careful in these times."
"Father," she pressed, "Are they really gassing Jews? Are they building crematoria for the
living at Erfurt?" The professor replied. "Aren't the Jews the authors of the
Soviet Revolution? I would like to see them all . . . . all . . .
Solnishko, no: it's not true," he continued. "*Ach*, no, it is Soviet
propaganda, all lies, brazen lies. Just you look at what they say about me, us.
I wore a Ukrainian peasant shirt; that makes me a traitor? Beware, my girl."

Then Anastasia Filipovna, Nikolai's wife, Zina's mother,
entered the narrow, dark room. She turned, knelt, and kissed the icon,

hidden in a hole in the wall, hidden from the secret police of the atheist
Soviet state. Kneeling on a coarse straw mat, Zina's stern and unforgiving
mother prayed for the dead and a few of the living. From those
Orthodox Christian lips, Zina first heard the word *zhid*. There are
not to be boys to see Zina. But her father winks, and Zina sees the young Nikolai
on the sly. She asks him about the Jews. He laughs and says, "You don't
need to go to Hitler's Germany to see maltreated Jews; Ukraine's
bloody pogroms under the Tsars and even the Soviets wiped as many,
I'd say, out. But forget about the Jews; the Germans are coming back."

Tired and beaten by the Russian winter, a ragtag and frostbitten
German foot army begins its retreat; the soldiers march into
Zina's home town, into Nikolai's home; like a wildfire. the messages flame:
"They are shooting any man who resists! Soldiers, hide!"
Nikolai hides his uniform; Anastasia kisses her cross.

A Ukrainian neighbor, a friend, is working for the Germans;
Kneeling, Anastasia begs him to take her family. Young Nikolai and his
brother, sister, mother watch; Zina points to Nikolai and
cries out, "He is a mechanic"; the Germans needed mechanics.
They take Zina and Nikolai's family, and shoot the other men.

Kalinivka 1943

(Note: We cannot write epic poetry here. Here the muse of the aberrant, a Gorgon, raises her head and breaks everything down.)

Starving and cold, the retreating mob, not an army anymore,

German and Ukrainian, women and men, hobbles to the West,

stops at Kalinivka. In spring, white cornflowers dance over the mounds of the

round mass graves; teenagers make love on the grassy knolls.

Now, the mounds are covered with snow; if you listen, you can hear

Hilda, Ruth singing; Schlomo, big, strong, boasting;

in the spring, their Jewish cells cling to the roots of

dandelions, cling to the young sparse trees.

The young Ukrainians make love on the grassy knolls;

beneath, one, two, six, ten skeletons lie with bullet holes in their

skulls, a quick death; the SS call it a waste of ammunition;

in other knolls, Jews just suffocate, buried alive.

Zina and Nikolai make love on the icy mounds.

Winter now deepens; with freezing bare hands, the collaborator-slaves

Zina and Nikolai, carry cold metals, the engines of war, and they

pull, push, and fall. Ammunition and guns freeze. Rare torn makeshift cloths,

needed for cold bodies, cold hands and cold feet, are wrapped

around frostbitten fingers; the German troops march on. In the evening,

fire and some rest. Tonight, there is a cold vat of potatoes fouled by kerosene, rank, but plentiful; there is no fuel to heat, and the ally-slaves eat.

Next, Poland; Rubenstein's *Polonaise* playing day and night at its invasion;
its cavalry, praying for rain, hoped to encircle the German tanks, to mire
them down in the mud. Sad for the brave resistance, it was dry as bone.
Brave Poland, but the Warsaw Ghetto held out under worse bombardment
longer than that country did; teenage Jewish girls with sticks against tanks,
boys with bricks.

Prymsl 1943

The retreating German army camps at Prymsl, where the railroad
is haunted by deported Jews. Volodya, Nikolai's brother, and Zina's father
are trained to be guards. What did Ukrainian guards do? At the rail stations,
where departing Jews are beaten, stripped, and robbed, then pushed into
crowded boxcars, and emerge at their destinations, concentration camps,
dizzy from the dense human sweat, and are again beaten, stripped and robbed
(by whom?).
Zina and Nikolai walk on the train tracks where the boxcars once rolled,
as Anastasia, Zina's mother, learns to work at the railroad, too.

As the troops march toward Germany, they grow bolder, stronger, sentimental
for home. What is the status of Nikolai and his kin, of Zinaida and her parents?

They are still *untermenschen*, underlings, but not quite as low as the Jews.
They are permitted to serve, like horses, and are kept well just the same.
And the Ukrainian *untermenschen* seek to serve well, for survival, for reward.

Erfurt 1943

On German soil, they come to Erfurt. Here the ingenious weapon of war,
the crematorium, is built. No need to waste bullets or rope to kill the *Juden*;
a pellet of cyanide and fifty are dead. The finest crematoria are built in Erfurt,
sturdy, brick. And here, Volodya and Nikolai *père* will be tested at last,
will work at the railroad. A staging camp will determine which Jews
will live to work, and which will be killed today.

The boxcar decelerates into the station, and stops;
human stench, offal and sweat, pours from the cracks of the doors.
Dirty Jews, the German officer in charge of the Slavic kapos says.
The doors open; men, women, and children spring forth.
As they have been taught, Volodya and Zinaida's father swing their clubs,
as the Jews cry, "But why?" and "There has been a mistake . . . ."
"Take off your clothes," Volodya orders; Zina's father beats
those who hesitate. Nikolai *père* collects up bracelets, rings, and watches,
and Volodya collects the furs. Soon everyone is naked; a stifled sob
from the Jews is met with a club.

The German officer comes to the front. Efficiently, he sifts through the naked horde.
"To the left, *bitte*," he says kindly to the old, sick, and very young
"to the right," he says quietly to others. The ones on the left cry out for their kin.
"Forward, please," the German officer says, and marches them away, never to return.
A mother screams for her son and is bludgeoned to death.

The crowd on the right are given prisoner garb and marched back on to the train.
It departs with its lightened freight, men in one car and women in the next.
Volodya turns the jewelry, gold, and fur over to the officer.
Bitte, he says quietly, and gives Volodya and Nikolai *père*
each a small gold filling from a tooth. The fillings are exchanged for food;
the Ukrainians know the Germans will not let them keep the gold.
A soldier gives a loaf of bread and a side of ham; the family eats for a week.

No longer hungry, they march to their destination, Nordhausen. The soldiers whisper,
"Here they make the secret weapons that will help us win the war."
The Ukrainians listen, understand nothing. There is a camp in the center
of the industrial complex called Dora. "There you will be gassed
with the Jews and the Russian POWs if you fuck up," a German lieutenant
laughs. Zina tries to laugh, but cannot.

"Listen," the German lieutenant says, sidling closer to her. "You speak good
German and you are not hard to look at. You can be a translator on the work gangs."
Like the SS lightning, the idea charges her brain. *I do have good German,*

she thinks, *and Russian, and Ukrainian. And Mama knows Yiddish and Polish as well.* "Yes," she tells the German officer. "I will translate for you. But not like those Ukrainian women who ride on your carts, the ones you call translators, who only translate their butts from one German to another. I will be a real translator, a linguist." And she smiled at him, a genuine smile.

Was bargaining possible in hell? Could the enslaved make terms?
It happened to one out of 20,000,000, with the frequency
of miracles. And these were often lost among death.

Nordhausen and Dora, 1943

And they marched to the Harz Mountains. Here were doors of death:
The enormous concentration camp Nordhausen with a dozen subcamps,
Dora and more small concentrated lagers, the prisoners too sick
for any other camp. And no one knows all there is to know about it,
not even the *Lagerfuhrer*. They are making, whispered the Germans,
the secret missiles, the V2 here. Or have they stopped –
sabotage from the prisoners hanged today?

Here the work is hard; more *haftlinge*, prisoners, die here than in other camps,
and the kapos are cruel: prisoners themselves, they work hard
to please their German captors, for alcohol, for tobacco, for

69

quarters with family, not those fit for pigs. They kapo for food.
They squeeze and pummel and starve the prisoners in their keep.
Here, Zina and her father and mother and her lover Nikolai
and his brother and mother will all be kapos, prisoner-guards,
the German lieutenant has promised his Ukrainian girl.

Here at the gates of Nordhausen . . . *Stop. Stop, before you,*
poet, narrator, comfortable and well-fed, American-born,
born many years after the war, stop before you enter these gates
Stop. Start with this: What did those gates look like? Do you know?
Were they wood, or fence with barbed wire around?
Were they brick, or walls of stone?
Hear me, spoiled woman who has never known hunger or war:
I am the voice of Dora, your prosopopaia.
Do you know how little you know?
Conscience, I do not even know what the gates of that lager looked like;
I don't know even that much about the camp.
Nor did I know my folk were kapos; many Slavs were slaves,
slave labor. I know some of what has passed
till now from stories, blurred with age.
I know Volodya and my grandfather, père Nikolai,
guarded railroads, but did they guard and torture Jews?

Was what I wrote above true? I don't know. So how can I tell you more?

I won't go into that camp. Would you, reader, voluntarily?

But . . .

But the stories draw me back, revealed episodically, not chronologically, like traumatic memory—or people hiding crimes.

My mother said that in Nordhausen, they worked in tunnels, were transported through tunnels but to work on what, she didn't know. Yet, she seemed guilty, but all survivors do. "I opened a gate," she said once. For whom?

Another time, she told how a resistance fighter came to her, said, "Just look away."

What was she watching, guarding, my gatekeeper Mom, whom?

Conscience: Larissa, Lora as your parents called you, you were always an evil child, like the little Nazis and Communists who turned in their parents. Why must you make your family evil?

Your childhood trauma, some ill-considered cruel words, and this your revenge? To call your parents Nazi collaborators, when they only were slaves?

Return to your childhood, to your comfortable middle-class home. . . .

Maspeth, 1972

One weekend dinner, now in Queens, New York, where my family are successful immigrants, with a house and a car, the relatives bring an article from *Life*. Aerial shots, closeups of the streets and bombed buildings of Nordhausen.

"This is where we were," they said in wonder, seeing the place for the first time.

But back first. . .

The Displaced Persons Camp, Harz Mountains 1945–1950

After the liberation of Nordhausen, there were DP camps, displaced persons' camps. There, Russians and Ukrainians who wouldn't go back to Stalin's Soviet Union waited for repatriation. My sister is born there.

My sister's godfather, my mother's *cum*, asked my father, "Kid, you want to drive a truck?" and *na levo*, my father drove a black-market truck for Anatoly, the potbellied brains of the operation.

But this could not last; they had to emigrate. In the Ukraine, they would be imprisoned; Stalin permitted no Soviet to be taken prisoner; the last bullets, he ordered, should be for them, suicide before capture. They would be tried and sent to Gulag. Where would they go? Australia?

The Lower East Side and Brooklyn 1955

A stroke of luck: McCarthyist anticommunism ironically opens the U.S. gates to Slavs who will not go home. And as they always had, together, they came to New York via Boston, working together to escape Williamsburg and the rats of Avenue B.

Queens 1957

When my family bought the house in Queens, there was a flag pole on the front lawn. Nikolai dug it out. "I've had enough of flags," he said.

Father, requiescat in pace.
Mama, rest in peace, as you could not while alive.
Volodya, who always wanted so to talk about the war, THE war, be still.
Dedya Kolya, père Nikolai, who never shaved his Hitler mustache, you fed me.
Anastasia, hard-handed grandmother, you brushed my hair, took me to church.
You all raised me: Who am I to cast you down?
Never hungry, thanks to you.
Never in fear of my life.
Always comfortable, thought of by everyone as rich for my clothing and my schools.
Any trouble always of my own making.

Who I am to judge? I am no one.

They say never forget, but today I say I don't know and forgive.

But . . .but . . .

There . . . .

My father gave bread to a Jewess in Nordhausen. Why would he have extra bread?

Was it extra bread?

Frau, bitte, pan, brot, my mother said the Jews said to her.

And my mother in the camps pregnant, and not married. She asked to be married. *Live together like dogs,* she said the Germans said. (Would Jews even ask?)

She told the anecdote of how a black American soldier, liberator of the camp, took Zina and Nikolai to the reluctant German burghers and said, "You marry dese people." It was a Zina lie, a fantasy anecdote for the *Reader's Digest* that she wished described her life.

Delivered of a son in the DP camp, she was abandoned by Nikolai for a lithe woman called Marusya. Nikolai's mother, Pasha, broke them up. Zina proudly tells the tale of how Pasha confronted Nikolai: "Take the garbage out!"

The baby boy dies; Zina mourns, beating her head against the grave; Nikolai drinks and finds women.

They were not German.

Not Jewish.

In between.

Primo Levi said the Ukrainians in the camps were crueler than the Germans. But that was the chemist suicide's say-so. (You are talking about my mother, Primo! Take it back!)

Today

I won't go through the Nordhausen gate. I choose not to go. But I dream sometimes of a white room without doors, with no escape. I think of what my captors might like. I cheerfully offer sadistic sexual scenarios, Greek and Roman, from the literature I know, and hope others take the tortures. According to my subconscious, I would be the first to do anything to save my skin.

Hannah Arendt coined the phrase "the banality of evil" watching Eichmann on trial in Israel. She marveled at the ordinariness of the war criminal, lacking in all satanic genius. My parents were a bookkeeper and a machinist with two children, pets, and a house in Queens. I wondered that they did not suffer horrible flashbacks of atrocities against Jews in the camps. Had they not seen any? Or was this like Tony Soprano ice-picking a man to death and then going home to eat lasagna?

For some people, other people's pain, however gruesome, doesn't register. Did they say, it was war, and shrug away their actions at Kalinivka with its mass graves, Prysml with its deportations, Erfurt with its staging camp, and the sick Jewish labor and crematoria at Dora?

Voice of Dora: What would you do, Larissa, to stay alive? To keep your children alive? Tell me: Is complicity possible without choice?

My mother telling the story (real life was never good enough for her) of how her father was looking for food and how a German turned to shoot him. My mother said she said, "The next bomb that hits will fall on your house," and the German lowered his gun. She also said that the German dogs would not attack her, animals loved her so.

Quietly, one night not long before her death: "You know that we did not want to work for the Germans," she said.

Earlier, sotto voce: "I opened a gate."

"A member of the Resistance told me to look away and I did."

The brutality, I always thought, was Stockholm Syndrome, over-identification with the oppressor. Was I right?

Dedushka (still Dedushka and not "my grandfather") wore a Hitler moustache in the United States, perhaps to keep the fond memories alive of "what we were?"

Coincidence that they chose to live among Germans, in the then German Maspeth neighborhood? Stockholm syndrome?

My parents were not true anti-Semites, just opportunistically so, unlike my more talented and accomplished grandparents, my grandmother whom I knew better than my Ded, my Ded who died when I was four. My grandmother used the word *zhid* whenever she encountered a Jew (but you don't need to be a Nazi to do that).

The banality of evil.

The sin of judgment, mine. The accused are not here to defend themselves, to say, *from scraps you have woven condemnations, blackened our name. Because we could be cruel, but lavished you with food and money, what we wished we had in the war. The best schools. Museums, opera, theater, ballet.*

Shall I erase this file? Tear the paper to bits, consign the Word file to Trash, and then erase it again? I can't. It would remain on the hard drive of my mind forever, urging me to tell, speak (snitch).

They are not here to defend themselves. Neither are the Jews.

There Was No Crematorium at Dora, my mother said. But she said earlier that the Russian POWs were gassed. *(Mama said.)*

Crematorium Limerick

> My mother said (dear, dearest Mum)
> In camp Dora was no crematorium.
> Then, she said that there was, so,
> As a guard there she would know;
> But truth telling just hurt her poor tum.

My mother said.

Previously, she had said, "Jews were not the only people who suffered in the camps." Why was my mother lying about the crematorium at Dora, the concentration camp within the labor camp of Nordhausen, part of the Buchenwald camp complex, an extension camp also known as Dora Mittelbau?

They called me Lora at home, never Larissa or the Russian Lara. Lora, rhymes with Dora.

Prisoners often knew little about their camps, kapos too. "We did not know what we were doing," my mother said, and those were the truest words she ever uttered.

Your (sexually undisciplined) father used to give bread to the Jewish woman who cleaned the barracks (and got what in return?)

Do slave laborers have cleaning ladies? And extra bread?

There is a reticence—not reticence, but inner taboo—on speaking of parental abuse: Honor thy mother and father and don't talk about rape, either. These internalized systems protect the abusers and screw the child. Fuck the victim.

Through the camps, on their retreat with the German Army through Kalinivka, Prymsl, Erfurt, my parents were at each camp (good camps, my mother called them) about two years after the worst atrocities.

Their shoes, lousy straps of cloth. They were not rich. Therefore, they were slave labor, not collaborators.

"The West Ukraine collaborated, not us," my mother said.

Slave labor. As though seized by an idea, my mother called out one night, "We were SLAVE LABOR!" A new idea, apparently. A victim's realization of abuse, or another cover up? Victims are fucked up. It took me, after all, until I was 36, to realize that the savage pummeling by a drunken man that I screamed and cried through at age 13 was rape, not consensual sex.

The barracks at Nordhausen were bombed. The story my mother told was that my father's sister Lena did not want to go to work. Pregnant Zina leaned down to get Lena's shoes, "the broken straps we used for shoes" and Pasha said, "Lena, aren't you ashamed? Pregnant Zina is getting your shoes," and Pasha bent down on the floor and Lena bent down on the floor, and "Wham! Just then the bombs hit the barracks. And only our quarters still stood."

Would Jews have lived with family? Were they simply better-treated Nazi slaves?

Drunk, one day, my father said of my grandfather that "he told a lot of lies."

Grandfather, of the tiny Hitler mustache, whom my mother said once had said that people were not to be judged by their color "whether they were black or white or purple polka dot."

My mother, let's face it, told a lot of lies.

There

The camps call. A woman whose man's name was also Nikolai, my mother said, used to call him with loving diminutives, *Kolya? Nikolka?* then *Nikolai!* and finally, *Nikolai chorto krokodil!* Nikolai, you devil crocodile. "It made us laugh," my mother said.

Later, the same woman, trapped under the wall of a bombed building, called out to Nikolai again, who, true to form, never came.

"Your father pulled her out; she had no legs and died soon after."

My father referred to my sister and me as *schweinerei*. Did he call Jews that?

The "good camps," as my mother called Kalinivka, Prymsl, Erfurt: Good for whom?

I glimpse inside Nordhausen and I hear again: "I opened a gate." This was recounted in a still small voice, not the braggadocio my mother usually used to lie.

A psychiatrist once said that I was motivated by responsibility. I am responsible for telling this story, responsible to the truth. And those I accuse are not here to defend themselves, and I must.

Conscience, voice of Dora, sing to Calliope and me: Think that the quiet acceptance of the monstrosities of their past was your parents' way of sparing you, a type of stoicism unknown by your generation. The austere offices of love as they worked at jobs they could not have liked to buy you bicycles and books. You are not a mother, Lora, and cannot know what parents will do for their children in a camp, yes, even kill.

I hear my mother's voice. Quietly. "We did not want to work for the Germans."

"Yes," my mother said late in life, "we were for the Germans. We thought the atrocities described were Stalin's propaganda. But then we saw what they were doing to children, and we said no."

But by then, Mama, it was too late, wasn't it?

"I opened a gate."

"A member of the Resistance told me to look away and I did."

My mother opened a gate. Helped the resistance.

Under fire, my father pulled a woman from the rubble.

They buried their first born in the DP camps, raised my sister there.

At the end of a war, everybody is starving, everyone is a prisoner, everyone is a Jew.

And complicity is not possible without choice.

Zina Nikolayevna Gnatchenko, Nikolai Fyodorovich Shmailo, thank you for surviving the war. Thank you for giving me life.

Rest in peace, Papa, Mama, Babushka, Dedushka.

Rest in peace.

EPILOGUE

TRAUMATIC MEMORY

Traumatic stories of traumatic events change depending upon the listener's as well as the teller's preparedness to accept the import of what has happened. This is true for me and my experience of my parent's involvement in the Holocaust and the Nazi camp system. Here was my understanding after interviewing my mother, who found it difficult to provide a chronological account; in 1992, I pieced the following poem together via family legends and these talks.

HOW MY FAMILY SURVIVED THE CAMPS

Was micht nicht umbringt, macht mich starker:
What does not kill me makes me stronger.
Nietzsche said this about other things
Not this.

How did my family survive the camps?
Were they smarter, stronger than the rest?
Were they lucky?
Did luck exist in Dora-Nordhausen,
Auschwitz and Bergen-Belsen?

How did my family survive?
They were young, my mother and father, in 1943
Twenty years old when taken as slaves.
No one knew my father was a soldier, a communist
So he was not shot
Or taken to be gassed.
My grandmother said quickly to the Germans
He is a mechanic; they needed mechanics
My grandmother, Soviet businesswoman
Begged and bribed the Ukrainian kapos
Begged and bribed the Germans, not SS
They took my father, son of a commissar
And shot the other men.

How did my family survive?
They offered no resistance
Did they collaborate?
Is complicity possible without choice?

They marched to Germany, working
Following the German army
Following the front
Digging trenches, carrying metal
These were the good camps, Kalinivka, Pyrmsl

There was still food:
My mother recalls eating an entire vat of potatoes
Fouled by kerosene, discarded by the Germans, not SS.

The treatment was not cruel, comparatively, not cruel:
In 1944, the Germans
Were as afraid of the Russian front
As the prisoners were of Germany
And of the other camps.
Where they went nonetheless
Where they were sent nonetheless.

How did they survive Erfurt, the selection?
My mother spoke good German
I see her now at the staging camp
Her keen wit dancing around the SS
Like her young Slavic feet
She was young and good-looking
Thin but good-looking
And the SS liked the Ukrainian Frauen.
On the cattle car to Dora
To the chimneys of that camp

My mother rode with her family intact
Thinner but intact
And ready for work.

How did my family survive?
Was it luck?
In Dora-Nordhausen
Where the air smelled of shit and gas
Where the sun rose but never shone
Was there luck?

The boxcar stopped
At the Nordhausen factory
The way out through the crematorium chimney in Dora
Here, my grandmother learned languages
Wstavach, Stoi, Ren, Schwein, Halt!
In Dora, where not to understand an order meant death
My grandmother learned six languages; after six months
My family could work, hide and ask for bread
In all the languages of Europe.
They learned English the same way.

How did my family survive?
When the Americans came, with chocolate and blankets
My father, six-foot-one
Was one hundred and twenty pounds
And still we were rich, my mother interjects,
Rich compared to the Jews.
A few months longer, though, a few months longer
We would not have been alive.

How did my family survive?
My grandfather, a teacher
Told this story:
When the Americans came and saw the camp
They invited the people to loot the nearby towns
Take anything, the well-fed soldiers said
My grandfather stood and spoke: We are not animals, he said
But we were, my father interrupts, we were.

How did my family survive?
Survive is not the right word.
I'm alive, my father would say, alive
Alive because I did not die; others died.

Keep breathing, he encouraged me in difficult times,
Keep breathing.

In 1996, I answered what I deemed a serendipitous advertisement from Elie Wiesel, the famed Nazi hunter and author of the Holocaust memoir, *Night*. He was seeking an assistant; why not me? Armed with this poem, I set out.

Came time for the interview, I was disappointed to find that I would be meeting with Wiesel's wife. I spoke of my relatives' experience and read my poem.

Mrs. Wiesel was silent for a moment. She then cocked her head and said deliberately: "If your parents weren't Jewish, what were they doing in the camps?"

I was taken aback by what I thought was the ignorance of the question. "Like many Slavs, they were slave labor in the camps," I replied.

Mrs. Wiesel paused and asked again: "If your parents weren't Jewish, what were they doing in the camps?"

The interview came to an uncomfortable close. *Bimbo!* I thought. *So uneducated as to the variegated makeup of the camps: Slavs, disabled people, homosexuals, French resistance. If only I could have talked to Wiesel himself; surely that fabled man would understand the poem.*

I never heard from the Wiesels but a question had been planted: What were my parents doing in the camps? What did Ukrainians do in the camps?

Primo Levi, the chemist suicide, wrote in his Holocaust memoir, *Survival in Auschwitz* (renamed by the English publisher from the Italian title, *Se queso è un mom*, "If This Is a Man") that the camp overseers, the Ukrainian *kapos*, were often crueler than the Germans as they sought to curry favor with their masters. And Mrs. Wiesel had recognized me as Ukrainian American. Was my family less than heroic in the camps?

All the books I had read so voraciously flooded back: *The Diary of the Lodz Ghetto; Night;* Levi; *The Rise and Fall of the Third Reich;* Tadeuzs Borowski's autobiographical short stories, *This Way for the Gas, Ladies and Gentlemen* (the original title in Polish is *Pożegnanie z Marią,* "Farewell to Maria"). How Viktor Frankl's *Man's Search for Meaning* became my guiding philosophy—how moved I was by his *zazen* sight of a bird in the concentration camp, how it recalled a larger and more benevolent universe and inspired Frankl to choose a humane response to the inhuman milieu surrounding him. *The Diary of a Young Girl,* Anne Frank's story read countless times. And the films: *Sophie's Choice,* written and directed by Alan J Pakula, in which a mother must choose which one of her two children shall live, and which one shall die at the selection, and Steven Spielberg's film *Schindler's List; Cabaret* and the chilling rendition of "Tomorrow Belongs to Me." The heroism of the gentile helpers; surely my family ranked among them?

A darker writing took shape at the turn of the 21st century:

KALINIVKA, PRMYSL, DORA

Kalinivka

Kalinivka, Kalinivka: The ground over the mass graves is hard, the soft grass grows. The Ukrainian Guard, boy and girl, make love, happy to be alive. In the Ukraine, collectivized, they walked on corpses. And the Germans alone protest, her father tells the girl. Siberia, purges. Like the Irish, their parents collaborate; Hitler fights the Russian and English masters of their rural lands. Now here, Kalinivka. The mass graves crack with green life. 1941 is forgotten in the summer of '43. She is 19, pregnant soon.

Prymsl

By 1943, the ghetto holds the few not deported, living in tunnels, basements, caves, the hiding ones, the ones who know. All the rest to camps in Poland, Germany, or dead. The boy no longer likes the girl, but through her, he got his Kapo job. Even his mother says, marry. Have a child. The female Kapo bears a boy through the camps, Prymsl, through the unknown tombs of Poland, the unmarked graves, the walls marked with Jewish blood, the bloody broken nooses, the dark rain. She wants the boy to marry her, he makes excuses, says, the Germans won't permit. That the child will die soon after the war, that she will beat her head upon the grave until it bleeds, that sorrow is unknown. The death of the Jewish children is unseen. Poland is always green.

Dora

Germany, Harz Mountains. The Germans turn now, now SS. The war is failing. Fewer the slaves to command, the girl, heavy with child, translates, working, starving, carried in rail carts for miles to build the V-2s. A rachitic Jewess cleans the barracks, the boy's eye turns, with pity, with lust; he gives her bread. From Erfurt to the extension camp, Buchenwald's new Dora, Nordhausen. Here they spare the rope to hang. All are hungry, the Germans too. The Allies bomb the industrial camp. Liberation. Rows of corpses, the eternal rows, line Nordhausen. The Germans are forced to respect the dead. Kalinivka, Prymsl, the unseen dead, now here in respectful symmetry, no longer piled in heaps, but rectangular, marked. The flowers grow, the burghers sing, "After every December, there comes a new spring."

There came a day when denial popped like a soap bubble, quietly, imperceptibly. My mind simply nodded assent: "Oh."

Since writing this book. I have learned not to judge my family. I don't know much of anything, for all the reading, of what I would do to survive. Don't judge my family—you don't know either.

ACKNOWLEDGMENTS

Bosch and Bruegel Poems (anthology, ed. David Sullivan): "Fall of Icarus"

Choice Words: Writers on Abortion (Haymarket Books 2020, anthology, ed. Annie Finch): "Abortion Hallucination"

Dispatches from the Poetry Wars: "American Life," Parts of a Flower," "Schooling," "Set of Examples and Nonexamples," "Spectacle Is the Fundamental Principle of Fascist Art"

Eco-Poetry: "Degree," "Plate Histrionics," "A Sonnet Affected by Climate Change"

Eoagh: "Anna Karenina," "Clad, Clawed, Clandestine Eagly Pig," "Razor"

Journal of Poetics Research: "An old red tree, dry . . .," "This is the rupture of heart . . .", "Catrain," "Cis Boom Trans," "Frog Prayer," "Spectrum Sells Out"

KGB Lit: "Anna Karenina: #MeToo"

ShadowKraft (Bengali-English journal): "Adoption"

Shrew: "&"

St. Petersburg Review: "New Life 7: Mistranslation of Joseph Brodsky with Addenda," "*Kompromat*"

"Sibyl" is featured in the film, *Sibyl, by Larissa Shmailo* by Tiziana Rinaldi: https://vimeo.com/132761090

Big Bridge, War Papers (ed. Halvard Johnson): "Kalinivka, Prmysl, Dora" (in "Traumatic Memory")

About the Author

Larissa Shmailo is a poet, novelist, translator, editor, writing coach, and critic. Shmailo's most recent book is the *Writing Resilience Workbook*. Her latest novel is *Sly Bang* (Spuyten Duyvil); her first novel is *Patient Women* (BlazeVOX). Her poetry collections are *Medusa's Country* (MadHat), *#specialcharacters* (Unlikely Books), *In Paran* (BlazeVOX), the chapbook *A Cure for Suicide* (Červená Barva Press), and the e-book *Fib Sequence* (Argotist EBooks). Her poetry albums are *The No-Net World* and *Exorcism*, for which she won the New Century Best Spoken Word Album award. Shmailo's work has appeared in the anthologies *Measure for Measure: An Anthology of Poetic Meters* (Penguin Random House), *Words for the Wedding* (Penguin), *Contemporary Russian Poetry* (Dalkey), *Choice Words: Writers on Abortion* (Haymarket) and many others. Shmailo is the original English-language translator of the first Futurist opera *Victory over the Sun* performed at the Los Angeles County Museum of Art, the Garage Museum of Moscow, the Brooklyn Academy of Music, and theaters and universities worldwide. Shmailo also edited the anthology *Twenty-first Century Russian Poetry* (Big Bridge Press) and has been a translator on the Russian Bible for the Eugene A. Nida Institute for Biblical Scholarship of the American Bible Society. Shmailo leads the workshop "Writing Resilience" for people affected by trauma, addiction, and/or mental illness. Her web site is www.LarissaShmailo.com.

OTHER BOOKS BY LARISSA SHMAILO

Writing Resilience Workbook (Patient Women Press, 2021)

Sly Bang (Spuyten Duyvil, 2018)

Patient Women (BlazeVOX [books], 2015). Semifinalist, Subito Press/University of Boulder Prose Competition.

Medusa's Country (MadHat Press, 2016)

#specialcharacters (Unlikely Books, 2014). Finalist, Elizabeth P. Braddock Award.

In Paran (BlazeVOX [books], 2009)

Fib Sequence (Argotist Ebooks, 2011)

A Cure for Suicide (Červená Barva Press, 2006)

From Pushkin to Pussy Riot: 30 Contemporary Voices on Russia and Politics (anthology co-edited with Philip Nikolayev, *Matter*, 2019)

Victory over the Sun by Alexei Kruchenych (Červená Barva Press, 2014)

Twenty-first Century Russian Poetry (anthology as editor-in-chief; Big Bridge Press, 2013)

Bibliography of Bible Translations in the Languages of the Russian Federation, Other Countries in the Commonwealth of Independent States, and the Baltic States. Eugene A. Nida Institute for Biblical Scholarship of the American Bible Society (pending publication)

RECENT TITLES FROM UNLIKELY BOOKS

Here, Which Is Also a Place by Mark DuCharme

Handling Filth: Simple Sabotage Field Manual by Jared Schickling

White Van by Meg Tuite

Flight Advice: a fabulary by Tobey Hiller

A Brief Conversation with Consciousness by Marc Vincenz

~getting away with everything by Vincent A. Cellucci and Christopher Shipman

fata morgana by Joel Chace

Typescenes by Rodney A. Brown

Political AF: A Rage Collection by Tara Campbell

The Deepest Part of Dark by Anne Elezabeth Pluto

Swimming Home by Kayla Rodney

Manything by dan raphael

Citizen Relent by Jeff Weddle

The Mercy of Traffic by Wendy Taylor Carlisle

Cantos Poesia by David E. Matthews

Left Hand Dharma: New and Selected Poems by Belinda Subraman

Apocalyptics by C. Derick Varn

Pachuco Skull with Sombrero: Los Angeles, 1970 by Lawrence Welsh

Monolith by Anne McMillen (Second Edition)

When Red Blood Cells Leak by Anne McMillen (Second Edition)

My Hands Were Clean by Tom Bradley (Second Edition)

www.ingramcontent.com/pod-product-compliance
Lightning Source LLC
Chambersburg PA
CBHW081006120626
46546CB00010B/3027